Live Action

Walking

Andrew Langley

Chrysalis Education

Distributed in the United States by
Smart Apple Media
2140 Howard Drive West
North Mankato, Minnesota 56003

Library of Congress Control Number: 2003116868

ISBN 1-59389-149-0

Editorial Manager: Joyce Bentley
Project Editors: Lionel Bender and Clare Lewis
Designer: Ben White
Production: Kim Richardson
Picture Researcher: Cathy Stastny

Produced by Bender Richardson White, U.K.

Printed in China

10 9 8 7 6 5 4 3 2 1

Words in **bold** can be found in Words to remember on page 31.

Picture credits
Corbis: 21 (Gallo Images), 27. Natural History Photo Agency: 19 (Ernie Janes). Digital Vision:
7, 9, 13. Rex Features Ltd: 4 (Stewart Cook), 12 (Henry T. Kaiser), 17 (Isopress), 20 (Alex Segre),
22 (Sipa), 23 (Palm Beach Post), 25 (Reso), 29 (Lehtikuva). RSPCA Photo Library: 11 (Mike
Powles), 15 (Andrew Mounter). Steve Gorton: 1, 6, 8, 10, 14, 16, 18, 24, 26. Stockbyte: 28.
Cover: Corbis (main image, front inset centre left), Steve Gorton (back, front insets far
left, far right), Digital Vision (front inset centre right). Illustration page 5: Jim Robins.

Contents

Moving with muscles

To walk, you move your legs with a swinging action. You lift one foot at a time, so you always have the other foot on the ground.

"Walking the dog" is good **exercise**—for people and for dogs.

The front muscle contracts (shortens and gets fatter), pulling the leg up.

The back muscle relaxes (gets longer and thinner), allowing the leg to rise.

Muscles work in pairs. One muscle contracts while the other muscle relaxes. In this way, muscles move the bones in your skeleton forward and back to help you to walk.

More than 20 pairs of muscles are used to walk.

You use **muscles** to make you walk. Muscles move the bones of your legs at the joints, such as your hips and knees.

Walking fast

To walk fast, take long strides—swing your legs far apart. Each foot lands on its heel and flattens. Then your toes act like springs to push you forward.

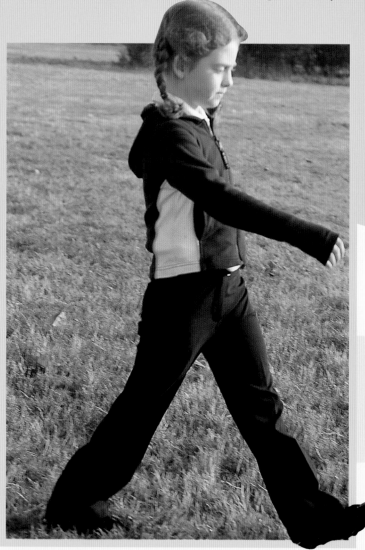

Swinging your arms to and fro as you walk will help you move faster.

Elephants can walk at 10 miles an hour (16 km/h)—faster than a person. They swing their long heavy trunks to help keep their balance as they move.

When an elephant walks, it always has at least one front leg and one hind leg on the ground at the same time.

An elephant has soft, padded feet, and makes very little noise when it walks.

Walking slowly

Sometimes you walk slowly. Perhaps you are tired, or you are carrying a heavy load of shopping. Or perhaps you are just not in a hurry.

People walk at a speed of about 4 miles an hour (6 km/h).

The wheels on a pram help you to push a load while you walk.

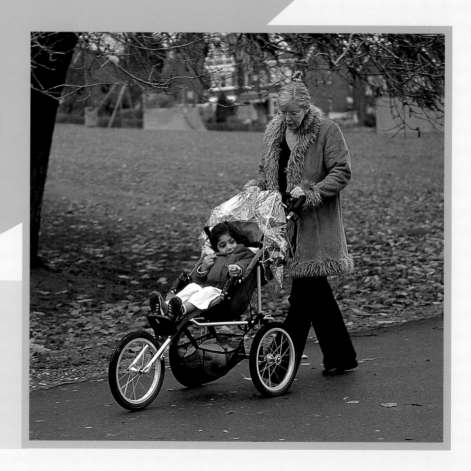

Tortoises and turtles walk very slowly. That is because they have a heavy shell to carry. Some walk at speeds of less than 250 yards (227 m) an hour.

Turtles use their **paddles** to pull themselves over the ground.

Creeping

To creep up on someone, crouch down as low as you can. Take care not to make a noise when you put your feet down.

Get down to the ground as low as you can to make yourself difficult to see.

As soon as a tiger sees its **prey**, it crouches down and creeps forward. It keeps low, so that it cannot be seen.

A tiger is hidden by long grass. When it gets close to its prey, it pounces.

When a tiger walks, its soft paws make no sound on the ground.

Wading

Walking through water is known as wading. Your muscles must work hard to push against the water.

If you put your feet down quickly you will make a splash!

Flamingos have **webbed** feet that stop them from sinking into the mud.

Flamingos' long, thin legs look like matchsticks. The birds often stand on just one leg.

Flamingos wade in **shallow** lakes and rivers, looking for food. They have long, thin legs that move easily through the water.

Walking uphill

Walking up a hill or stairs uses extra muscle power. As well as pushing you forward, your legs have to push you upward.

You use up more energy if carrying a load, such as a backpack, up hill.

To walk up to the top of the Empire State Building in New York you must climb 1576 steps.

The gecko can climb up walls and window glass. It can even walk upside-down across the ceiling!

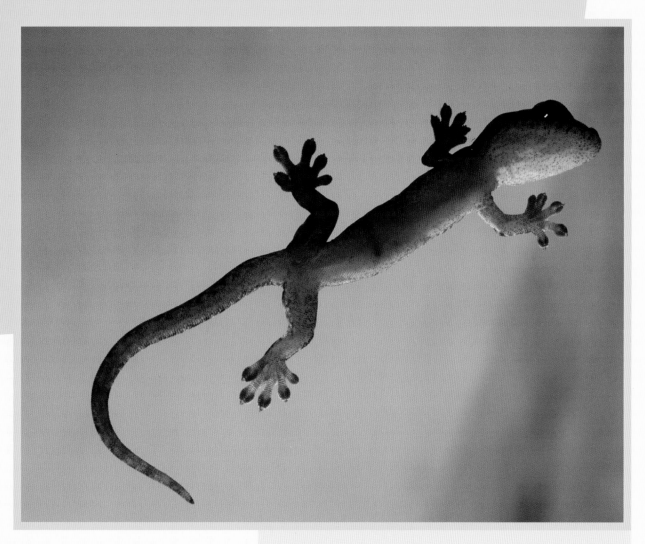

A gecko's feet have ridges with millions of tiny hairs that help the animal grip on surfaces.

Going down

Walk slowly and carefully down stairs or you will slip or trip over. Leaning back a little will help you stop falling forward.

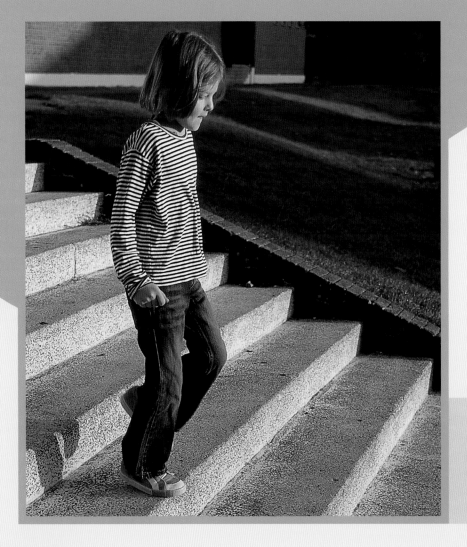

Moving your arms will help you to keep your balance.

Squirrels can walk down or up the trunks of trees. They use the toes of their feet to grip the trunks and stop themselves falling.

When a squirrel walks down a tree, it uses its tail to help keep its balance.

Treecreepers are birds that walk down tree trunks.

Walking tall

To walk upright, keep your back straight. You can "walk tall" to see further by stretching your neck, back, and legs, and by moving on the tips of your toes.

Walking on **tiptoe** raises your body so you can **see** over walls and fences.

Chimpanzees mostly walk on all fours. They will try to walk tall on their back legs when they want to scare off an enemy.

Most apes and monkeys live in trees, using their arms to swing from branch to branch.

Chimpanzees can look very threatening, but they do not often attack other animals.

Pushing

Pushing a "train" of trolleys is hard work. You have to use every muscle in your back, legs, and arms.

Strong people can push along objects weighing more than three times their own weight.

Lean forward so that your body pushes in the right direction.

The scarab beetle pushes along balls of **dung**. The beetle stands on two of its legs and pushes with the other four.

Scarab beetles normally walk on all six legs.

Pulling

In a tug-of-war, two teams take hold of opposite ends of a rope and pull backward. Each team tries to pull the other one toward it, using its weight and strength.

To win a tug-of-war, you have to pull the other team over a center line.

Reindeer can pull heavy loads. People use reindeer to pull sledges across the snow.

Reindeer have thick **fur**. They can walk in snow for hours without getting cold.

With their big **hoofs** and strong legs, reindeer can walk in deep snow.

Single file

People sometimes walk along in **single file** —one behind the other. The person in front decides where to go and how fast to walk. The others follow close behind.

Try marching in single file with everyone putting their left then right foot forward at the same time.

A long line of walking camels is called a "caravan."

Camels usually walk across deserts in single file. Adults go in the lead and at the back, with the young and their mothers in between.

Camels in a "caravan" often walk in step with each other.

Walking a long way

People enjoy walking long distances along coasts or over mountains. To do this you must be fit and healthy.

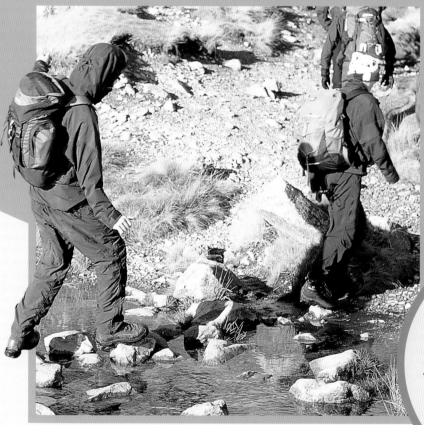

Long-distance walkers wear tough boots to help them to walk over all kinds of rocky and wet ground.

In the Olympic Games there are 12-mile (20-km) and 31-mile (50-km) walks. The 31-mile race takes about 3 hrs and 45 min.

As a giraffe walks, its head and neck bob up and down. If it kept its neck stiff, it would soon get a neck ache!

Giraffes walk up to 20 miles (32 km) a day to find food. They are so tall and have such big necks and bodies that their legs look too weak to support them—but they are not.

Resting

After a long walk, your leg muscles will feel tired and stiff. Your body will need a drink and food to replace the **energy** your muscles have used.

Once you sit down, your muscles will relax. Taking a cool drink will refresh you.

Animals need to rest after a long walk. They sit down while their body temperature cools down.

Dogs open their mouths and pant with their tongues out to help them cool down.

After exercise, a person's or animal's heartbeat and breathing slows. Sweating helps cool the body.

Facts and figures

The slowest mammal is the three-toed sloth of South America. It walks at just 125 yards an hour (0.16 km/h).

Some flies can taste with their feet. Blowflies can find out whether a food has sugar in it just by walking on it.

In a year, a caribou can walk more than 1400 miles (2250 km) across the Arctic, from south to north and back again.

The mudskipper—a fish that lives in central Africa—can stay out of water for several minutes, "walking" with its fins.

During an entire week (168 hours), a sloth spends only about 18 hours on the move—very slowly.

A lion usually walks about 6 miles (10 km) a day in search of prey.

The longest distance ever walked on a tightrope is 1550 yards (1400 m) by Chinese athlete Ahdili in 2000. The rope was stretched between two mountain peaks.

The youngest ever holder of a world athletics record was a walker. China's Wang Yan was only 14 when she broke the record for the 31¼-mile (50-km) walk.

Dung The droppings, or feces, of animals.

Energy The power that lets us exercise and move our bodies.

Exercise Regular activity, for example walking, running, swimming.

Fur The thick covering of hair on a some animals' bodies.

Hoof The horny nail that grows over the lower part of some animals' feet.

Joint A part of the skeleton where two bones meet.

Muscle A bundle of elastic-like fibers that can tighten or relax to move parts of our bodies.

Paddle Flat part of the body pushed against water to help swimming.

Prey An animal that is hunted and caught for food.

Shallow Not very deep water along the banks of a river, lake, or on the seashore.

Single file A single line of people or animals, one behind the other.

Tiptoe With the heel raised and only the toes and the ball of the foot touching the ground.

Webbed Wide, flat feet with stretches of skin between the toes.

Index